Rookie biographies®

Thurgood Marshall

By Christine Taylor-Butler

Subject Consultant
Susan Low Block, Professor of Law
Georgetown University, Washington, DC

Reading Consultant
Cecilia Minden-Cupp, PhD
Former Director of the Language and Literacy Program
Harvard Graduate School of Education
Cambridge, Massachusetts

Children's Press®
A Division of Scholastic Inc.
New York   Toronto   London   Auckland   Sydney
Mexico City   New Delhi   Hong Kong
Danbury, Connecticut

Designer: Herman Adler Design
Photo Researcher: Caroline Anderson
The photo on the cover shows Thurgood Marshall.

Library of Congress Cataloging-in-Publication Data

Taylor-Butler, Christine.
  Thurgood Marshall / by Christine Taylor-Butler.
    p. cm. — (Rookie Biographies)
  Includes index.
  ISBN 0-516-25015-9 (lib. bdg.)   0-516-27099-0 (pbk.)
  1. Marshall, Thurgood, 1908–1993—Juvenile literature. 2. United States
Supreme Court—Biography—Juvenile literature. 3. African American judges—
Biography—Juvenile literature. I. Title. II. Rookie biography
  KF8745.M34T39 2006
  347.73'2634—dc22   2005021635

1 2 3 4 5 6 7 8 9 10 R 15 14 13 12 11 10 09 08 07 06

Thurgood Marshall believed
that all people are equal.

4

Marshall was a lawyer and judge. He said the rights in the U.S. Constitution were for everyone in the United States. He helped change laws so that African Americans had the same rights as everyone else.

Marshall was born on July 2, 1908, in Baltimore, Maryland. He was the great-grandson of a slave.

A segregated theater in Baltimore

Baltimore was segregated. This meant that African Americans were not treated the same as white people.

African Americans could not shop in the same stores or swim in the same pools as white people. They could not live in white neighborhoods or attend white schools.

Marshall went to classes at Lincoln College in Chester, Pennsylvania, in 1925. All the students were African American.

All the teachers at Lincoln College were white. Marshall and his classmates tried to get Lincoln College to give jobs to African American teachers, too.

Marshall (back row, second from right) and other students at Lincoln College

Howard University

Marshall decided to become a lawyer after college. He wanted to help stop segregation.

Marshall hoped to attend the University of Maryland Law School. But African Americans were not allowed to go to that school.

Marshall went to Howard University Law School in Washington, D.C.

Marshall became friends with lawyer Charles Hamilton Houston. Houston told Marshall that many white judges and lawyers would not accept him.

Marshall knew he would have to work hard to show he was a good lawyer. In 1933, he graduated from Howard with the best grades in his class.

Charles Hamilton Houston

Marshall (left) with someone he helped during a court case in Baltimore

Marshall moved back home to Baltimore. He opened a law office there. Marshall helped many people. He even helped those who could not afford to pay him.

Marshall began working for
the National Association for
the Advancement of Colored
People (NAACP) in 1934.
The NAACP protects the rights
of African Americans.

Marshall and the NAACP tried
to change certain laws. They
wanted to stop segregation.
Marshall won most of the
cases he took to court.

Marshall (bottom, right) with other members of the NAACP and former first lady Eleanor Roosevelt (bottom, center)

Marshall worked hard to end an idea known as "separate but equal." People who agreed with this idea said that African American children had the same education as white children. Marshall knew that this was not true.

In 1954, he won a court case known
as Brown v. Board of Education.
"Separate but equal" was no longer
allowed in public education. African
American children could attend the
same schools as white children.

People all over the country
began noticing Marshall's skill
as a lawyer.

John F. Kennedy

In 1961, President John F. Kennedy wanted Marshall to be a judge on the U.S. Circuit Court of Appeals. This court hears cases that affect the nation.

Some politicians did not agree with Kennedy. They did not like Marshall's ideas about equal rights. But other policiticans respected Marshall. They supported him and helped him become a judge.

Lyndon Johnson (left) and Thurgood Marshall

In 1965, President Lyndon Johnson hired Thurgood Marshall as solicitor general. Marshall argued cases for the government in front of the U.S. Supreme Court. This is the highest court in the nation. Marshall won most of his cases.

In 1967, President Johnson wanted Marshall to be a justice, or judge, on the U.S. Supreme Court. Marshall became the first African American to sit on this court. He retired in 1991.

Marshall (bottom, left) with other U.S. Supreme Court justices in 1982

Thurgood Marshall fought hard for his beliefs. He worked to make sure that all people are treated equally.

Marshall died on January 24, 1993. People of all races continue to respect him.

Words You Know

Howard University

John F. Kennedy

justices

segregation

Thurgood Marshall

31

Index

About the Author

Christine Taylor-Butler is the author of more than twenty books for children. Because of Thurgood Marshall's efforts, she was able to attend the best schools in the country. She lives in Kansas City, Missouri, with her family.

Photo Credits